Test**Practice**

KS3 English

Collins · *do brilliantly!*

Test**Practice**

KS3 English

Test practice at its **best**

- **Alan Coleby**
- **Kate Frost**
- **Series Editor: Jayne de Courcy**

William Collins' dream of knowledge for all began with the publication of his first book in 1819. A self-educated mill worker, he not only enriched millions of lives, but also founded a flourishing publishing house. Today, staying true to this spirit, Collins books are packed with inspiration, innovation and practical expertise. They place you at the centre of a world of possibility and give you exactly what you need to explore it.

Collins. Do more.

Published by Collins
An imprint of HarperCollinsPublishers
77–85 Fulham Palace Road
Hammersmith
London
W6 8JB

Browse the complete Collins catalogue at
www.collinseducation.com

First published 2005
This revised edition published 2006

10 9 8 7 6 5 4 3 2 1

ISBN-13   978 0 00 72154 6
ISBN-10   0 00 721541 X

Alan Coleby and Kate Frost assert the moral right to be identified as the authors of this work.

British Library Cataloguing in Publication Data
A catalogue record for this publication is available from the British Library.

Acknowledgements
The extracts in the Reading Paper are reproduced from the following sources: *Tiger Woods* by Jack Clary (Tiger Books International, 1997); 'Through the tunnel' by Doris Lessing, in *Short Stories of Our Time*, ed. Douglas R. Barnes (Thomas Nelson and Sons, 1984); *Biology for Life* by M.B.V. Roberts (Thomas Nelson and Sons, 1981).
Photographs
Lew Long/CORBIS (p. 1); Tony Roberts/CORBIS (p. 2); Roy Morsch/CORBIS (p. 20).

Every effort has been made to contact the holders of copyright material, but if any have been inadvertently overlooked, the Publishers will be pleased to make the necessary arrangements at the first opportunity.

Edited by Jenny Draine
Production by Katie Butler
Design by Bob Vickers and Ann Paganuzzi
Printed and bound by Printing Express, Hong Kong

You might also like to visit
www.harpercollins.co.uk
The book lover's website

Contents

About the English National Test

When is the Test?

You will sit your English National Test in May of Year 9. Your teacher will give you the exact dates.

What does the Test cover?

The English curriculum is divided into three Attainment Targets:

En 1   Speaking and Listening
En 2   Reading
En 3   Writing

The Test covers Reading and Writing. It also covers the Shakespeare play you have studied in Year 9. Your teacher will have chosen one play out of a list of three, and there are two scenes in your play which you will have studied in great detail.

How many papers are there?

There are **three** Test papers:

- The Reading Paper, which is 1 hour 15 minutes.
- The Writing Paper, which is 1 hour 15 minutes.
- The Shakespeare Paper, which is 45 minutes.

Reading Paper

There are three reading passages, with questions in a separate booklet.

The passages are likely to be:

- a passage of prose which is non-fiction (it does not tell a story); it could be a biography or an autobiography, a leaflet, a newspaper article, a diary, a travel book, a magazine article, a letter or an advertisement

- a passage from a novel, short story or a poem

- another passage from any non-fiction book such as a textbook or an instruction manual.

You are allowed 15 minutes to read the three passages and 1 hour to write your answers.

This paper carries 32 marks.

Writing Paper

This paper has two tasks. The first is the **Longer Task**. You are advised to spend 45 minutes on this task, including using the Planning page, which will be opposite the page which tells you what the Longer Task is. You may be asked to write a story, or other form of writing, where you can be as imaginative as you like, and you can control much of the form in which you write. This is called an 'open' task.

This task carries 30 marks.

The second is the **Shorter Task**. You will have 30 minutes to spend on it, if you have taken 45 minutes on the Longer Task. The task will be a 'closed' or 'directed writing' task such as a letter, a newspaper report or a speech. Information will be provided for you to use in your writing. There is no Planning page for this task.

This task carries 20 marks.

Shakespeare Paper

There is **one task** on this paper about the Shakespeare play that you have studied. You have 45 minutes to answer it, including reading time.

Three plays are set each year. Two scenes from each play are for detailed study, and your teacher will have told you which these are. In 2006, these scenes are:

Macbeth

Act 2 Scene 1 (whole scene)
Scene 2 (whole scene)
Act 5 Scene 3 (whole scene)
Scene 4 (whole scene)
Scene 5 (whole scene)

Much Ado About Nothing Act 3 Scene 2 (whole scene)
Act 4 Scene 1 Lines 1–163

Richard III

Act 1 Scene 1 Lines 1–122
Act 3 Scene 7 Lines 94 to the end of the scene

There are passages from each scene printed on the question paper, and so you do not need to take a copy of the play into the Test.

This task carries 18 marks.

All students sit the same Test papers, and in English there is only one 'tier' resulting in the award of a level from 3 to 7.

How to do well in your Test

What is in this book

This book contains:

- complete Test Papers: Reading Paper, Writing Paper, Shakespeare Paper
- the Shakespeare plays and scenes for 2006
- detailed answers and marking guidance.

How to tackle the Reading Paper

You are given 15 minutes to read the three reading passages before you are allowed to write your answers. Make the best use of this time by reading all three passages thoroughly. Start thinking about the language, structure, purpose and audience of each passage. You won't see the actual questions until the 15 minutes' reading time is up, but you can begin to notice key features of the passages which may be of help when you do come to answer the questions.

The questions sometimes advise you to refer to words and phrases from the passage to support the ideas you write about in your answers. This means that you should give quotations from the passage. Quotations are words and phrases or whole sentences copied from the passage. You must remember to put inverted commas in front of and after the words you copy.

There are two things to remember about using a quotation. First, do not make it too long, usually no longer than a sentence. Second, do not just pick out any phrase or sentence, but make it refer to the ideas that you have expressed in your own words in your answer.

Remember that when examiners mark answers to the questions, they do not mark writing style – spelling, punctuation, grammar or paragraphing. They are concerned only with how well you have understood each passage and how relevant your answer is to the question.

Look hard at the mark allocation for each question as this will give you a guide as to how much to write. Spend longer on questions worth the most marks.

How to tackle the Writing Paper

You will be marked on 'Composition and effect' – how interesting what you write is, how appropriate the style you have chosen to write in is, and how well your writing engages the interest of your reader through your choice of vocabulary, etc.

You will also be marked on how well you express yourself: 'Sentence structure and punctuation' and 'Text structure and organisation'.

For the Longer Task, make sure that you use the planning sheet to plan your answer paragraph by paragraph. This planning is not wasted time as it will allow you to write your story more quickly. It will also ensure that your story is carefully constructed with a powerful opening and ending.

Allow at least five minutes to check through your writing when you have finished. Don't worry if you want to change a word – for example, you may want to change an adjective for a more powerful one or add inverted commas around speech. Do any crossings out as neatly as possible and you will not be penalised for this. In fact, you will be awarded higher marks if your editing of your writing has improved it – even if there are some crossings out.

On this paper there are two passages of about 50 or 60 lines each, selected from the two scenes that have been prescribed for detailed study. There may be a description of the context of the passages. There is then one task written in bold type, which refers to both passages.

You have 45 minutes to read the task and write your answer.

Tasks on the Shakespeare plays are usually of two types. The first is a 'critical discussion' question which will ask you about aspects of plot, character, meaning or language in the scenes:

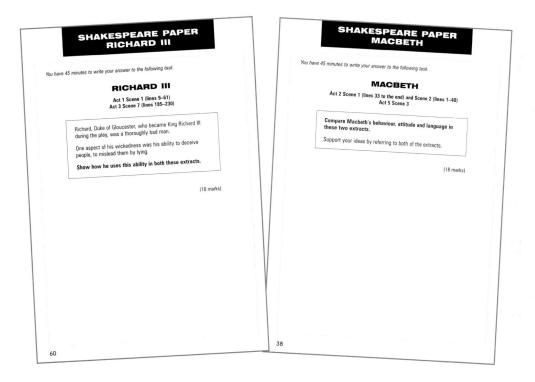

'Critical discussion' questions are the most frequently set. Remember that, in your answer to such a question, you must include quotations. Do not make these quotations too long (two or three lines at the most), and make them refer clearly to the ideas you express in your own words.

The second is an 'empathetic' question which will ask you to imagine that you are one of the characters and to write as if you were that person. With these types of question, it is important to show that you know what all the other characters think, do and say, as well as concentrating on your particular character.

How to work out your marks and calculate your level

Reading Paper

Add up the marks that you have achieved across all the questions on all three passages.

Writing Paper

For the Longer task, award yourself a mark within one of the mark ranges (see pages 23–30 for more details), after reading all the guidance and sample extracts.

Then do the same for the Shorter task using pages 31–36.

Shakespeare Paper

For whichever play you have chosen, decide which mark range your answer best fits, using the guidance and sample extracts provided. Then award yourself a mark within the range (see pages 44, 55 and 65 for more details).

The first table below gives the marks and levels for each paper. The second table gives your level for the three papers together, based on your total mark.

For technical reasons, the thresholds in the real tests for 2006 may be well below the overall thresholds given here.

Level	Reading	Writing Longer Task	Writing Shorter Task	Shakespeare
N	1–5	1–2	1–2	1–2
4	6–12	3–9	3–8	3–6
5	13–19	10–16	9–14	7–10
6	20–25	17–23	15–19	11–14
7	26–32	24–30	20	15–18

Level	Overall marks
3	4–14
4	15–38
5	39–62
6	63–84
7	85–100

Energy for life

Reading Paper

On the following pages you will find three reading texts:

1 An extract from the biography of the American golfer, Tiger Woods.

2 The conclusion of a short story by Doris Lessing.

3 *Getting Energy from Food*, an extract from a Science textbook.

Remember

- You have 15 minutes to read these texts.

- During this time you must not write or open the Answer booklet.

- At the end of 15 minutes you will have 1 hour to answer the questions.

This extract is from the biography of the young American golfer, Tiger Woods.

Without a doubt, Tiger Woods is the result of his father's plan to raise a golf champion. Earl Woods was a good athlete, whose principal claim to athletic achievement was as a baseball catcher during a short time at Kansas State University. Woods was a career Army man who worked his way through the ranks to the rank of lieutenant colonel when he fought in Vietnam. It was during his time in South East Asia that he met and married his second wife, Kultilda Punsawad. Six years later, their only son, Elrick, was born in Long Beach, California, on December 30, 1975.

Earl Woods had big plans for his new son, and they mostly revolved around the game of golf, to which Earl had been introduced a few years earlier. Earl has said that he was driven by the fact that as a black, he had long been denied access to the country-club world of golf. 'But I told myself that somehow my son would get a chance to play golf early in life.' So before Tiger was even one year old, his father would take him out to the garage and put him in his high chair or playpen, where the boy would watch his father pound ball after ball into a practice net and putt ball after ball into a cup.

His father has said that when Tiger was just ten months old, he took up a putter and gave a perfect display of the delicate art of putting a golf ball. When he was three, he won a pitch, putt and drive competition against ten- and eleven-year-olds.

But his father didn't limit his instruction to the sheer mechanics of golf. During his years as a Green Beret, he had learned a great deal about shaping a mind to cope with stress, and so he set out to mould his son's mind so that he could master the all-important skill of concentration. At age six, while Tiger was out in his family's garage hitting balls into the same net he had watched his father use, he

was also listening to subliminal messages on a tape recorder. His father had also 25
tacked messages of positive reinforcement to Tiger's desk in his room. Earl
Woods used a mixture of distractions that could cause a golfer's game to fall
apart. His father did everything, from making caustic remarks before Tiger was
set to tee off or sink a putt, to making noise at the top of his backswing. In Earl's
own words, he pulled 'every nasty, dirty, ungodly trick on him.' This went on until 30
his father was satisfied that he could endure anything on a golf course and not
crack.

While Earl handled the golf course and the playing schedule when his job
allowed, as well as juggling the family's financial resources to help maintain Tiger's
playing needs, his wife provided strength and stability at home. She not only 35
served as a taxi service to Tiger's midweek golf matches, but more importantly,
she also saw to it that he responded to all the demands of family life. She insisted
that he conduct himself properly, and particularly that he adhere to the
gentlemanly protocols of golf. At the same time, she taught him some of her own
toughness, driving home the point that when he was ahead in a match he should 40
not let up, but instead, try as hard as he could to overwhelm an opponent. Then,
when the match was won, he was to be a sportsman.

The 'tough love' that Earl used to shape his son's character was nothing more
than solid parenting. For example, in his very early years, Tiger was given a set of
shortened clubs and when he looked in the bag and didn't see a 1-iron, the 45
hardest club to hit, he asked to have one. He was told he was still too young to
generate enough clubhead speed to use it effectively; but a while later, he was out
on the driving range, using his father's 1-iron – which was almost as long as he
was tall – so effectively that there was little doubt he could handle it. His dad
promptly went out and bought him one. 50

In 1997, Tiger Woods took part in the U.S. Masters golf tournament. He
became the youngest ever to win the title as well as the first to win the first
major he ever played in as a professional. His twelve-stroke victory margin was
the largest ever at the Masters, and the largest in any major championship this
century. 55

When he sank his final putt to make par on the 18th, he spun around and
churned his arm up and down, his patented punctuation mark to signify that he
had achieved something special. A few moments later, he was in the embrace
of his parents, dissolving into tears as he hugged his father for nearly a half
minute. 'I think more than anything I was relieved it was over,' Tiger said later. 'I 60
think every time I hug my mom or pop after a tournament, it's over. I
accomplished my goal. And to share it with them is something special.'

When he talked by phone with President Bill Clinton a few moments later,
the First Golfer told him: 'The best shot I saw all week was the shot of you
hugging your dad.' 65

Conclusion of a short story by Doris Lessing

Jerry, a young English boy in South Africa, and a very good swimmer, longed to be accepted by a group of native boys. These boys were such good swimmers that they could dive to the sea bed and swim through a long tunnel, underneath a wide barrier rock, before surfacing the other side. Jerry wanted to show that he was as good as they were, by swimming through the tunnel.

But even after he had made the decision, or thought he had, he found himself sitting up on the rock and looking down into the water, and he knew that now, at this moment, when his nose had only just stopped bleeding, when his head was still sore and throbbing – this was the moment when he would try. If he did not do it now, he never

5   would. He was trembling with fear that he would not go, and he was trembling with horror at that long, long tunnel under the rock, under the sea. Even in the open sunlight the barrier rock seemed very wide and very heavy; tons of rock pressed down on where he would go. If he died there he would lie until one day – perhaps not before next year – those big boys would swim into it and find it blocked.

10   He put on his goggles, fitted them tight, tested the vacuum. His hands were shaking. Then he chose the biggest stone he could carry and slipped over the edge of the rock until half of him was in the cool, enclosing water and half in the hot sun. He looked up once at the empty sky, filled his lungs once, twice, and then sank fast to the bottom with the stone. He let it go and began to count. He took the edges of the hole in his hands and

15   drew himself into it, wriggling his shoulders in sideways as he remembered he must, kicking himself along with his feet.

Soon he was clear inside. He was in a small rock-bound hole filled with yellowish-grey water. The water was pushing him up against the roof. The roof was sharp and pained his back. He pulled himself along with his hands – fast, fast – and used his legs

20   as levers. His head knocked against something; a sharp pain dizzied him. Fifty, fifty-one, fifty-two…. He was without light, and the water seemed to press upon him with the weight of rock. Seventy-one, seventy-two…. There was no strain on his lungs. He felt like an inflated balloon, his lungs were so light and easy, but his head was pulsing.

He was being continually pressed against the sharp roof, which felt slimy as well as

25   sharp. Again he thought of octopuses, and wondered if the tunnel might be filled with weed that could tangle him. He gave himself a panicky, convulsive kick forward, ducked his head, and swam. His feet and hands moved freely, as if in open water. The hole must have widened out. He thought he must be swimming fast, and he was frightened of banging his head if the tunnel narrowed.

30   A hundred, a hundred and one…. The water paled. Victory filled him. His lungs were beginning to hurt. A few more strokes and he would be out. He was counting wildly; he said a hundred and fifteen, and then, a long time later, a hundred and fifteen again. The water was a clear jewel-green all around him. Then he saw, above his head, a crack running up through the rock. Sunlight was falling through it, showing the clean dark rock

35   of the tunnel, a single mussel shell, and darkness ahead.

He was at the end of what he could do. He looked up at the crack as if it were filled with air and not water, as if he could put his mouth to it to draw in air. A hundred and fifteen, he heard himself say inside his head – but he had said that long ago. He must go on into the blackness ahead, or he would drown. His head was swelling, his lungs cracking. A hundred and fifteen, a hundred and fifteen pounded through his head, and he feebly clutched at rocks in the dark, pulling himself forward, leaving the brief space of sunlit water behind. He felt he was dying. He was no longer quite conscious. He struggled on in the darkness between lapses into unconsciousness. An immense, swelling pain filled his head, and then the darkness cracked with an explosion of green light. His hands, groping forward, met nothing, and his feet, kicking back, propelled him out into the open sea.

He drifted to the surface, his face turned up to the air. He was gasping like a fish. He felt he would sink now and drown; he could not swim the few feet back to the rock. Then he was clutching it and pulling himself up on to it. He lay face down, gasping. He could see nothing but red-veined, clotted dark. His eyes must have burst, he thought; they were full of blood. He tore off his goggles and a gout of blood went into the sea. His nose was bleeding, and the blood had filled the goggles.

He scooped up handfuls of water from the cool, salty sea, to splash on his face, and did not know whether it was blood or salt water he tasted. After a time, his heart quieted, his eyes cleared, and he sat up. He could see the local boys, diving and playing half a mile away. He did not want them. He wanted nothing but to get back home and lie down.

In a short while, Jerry swam to shore and climbed slowly up the path to the villa. He flung himself on his bed and slept, waking at the sound of feet on the path outside. His mother was coming back. He rushed to the bathroom, thinking she must not see his face with bloodstains, or tearstains, on it. He came out of the bathroom and met her as she walked into the villa, smiling, her eyes lighting up.

'Have a nice morning?' she asked, laying her hand on his warm brown shoulder a moment.

'Oh, yes, thank you,' he said.

'You look a bit pale.' And then, sharp and anxious, 'How did you bang your head?'

'Oh, just banged it,' he told her.

She looked at him closely. He was strained. His eyes were glazed-looking. She was worried. And then she said to herself: 'Oh, don't fuss! Nothing can happen. He can swim like a fish.'

They sat down to lunch together.

'Mummy,' he said, 'I can stay under water for two minutes – three minutes, at least.' It came bursting out of him.

'Can you, darling?' she said. 'Well, I shouldn't overdo it. I don't think you ought to swim any more today.'

She was ready for a battle of wills, but he gave in at once. It was no longer of the least importance to go to the bay.

'Getting Energy from Food', an extract from a science textbook

Does food really contain energy?

We need energy to move, grow, mend our tissues when they are damaged, and just to keep ourselves alive. We get energy from our food. The energy contained in food used to be expressed in kilocalories, but this term has been replaced by kilojoules (kj). 4.2 kj of energy are required to raise the temperature of 1 kg of water through 1°C.

The amount of energy in a particular food depends on the substances which it contains. The three main kinds of food are carbohydrate, fat and protein. If we estimate the amount of energy in each of these, we can compare their energy values. Here they are:

Carbohydrate	1 gram contains 17 kj
Fat	1 gram contains 39 kj
Protein	1 gram contains 18 kj

Table 1 tells us how much energy there is in some everyday foods.

Table 1

	Kj per gram		Kj per gram
Margarine	32.2	White bread	10.6
Butter	31.2	Chips	9.9
Peanuts	24.5	Roast chicken	7.7
Milk chocolate	24.2	Eggs	6.6
Cake	18.8	Boiled potatoes	3.3
White sugar	16.5	Milk	2.7
Pork sausages	15.5	Bottled beer	1.2
Cornflakes	15.3	Boiled cabbage	0.34
Rice	15.0		

Thus, margarine and butter contain a lot of energy because they consist almost entirely of fat. At the other extreme, cabbage contains very little energy because it consists of a high percentage of water.

How much energy do we need each day?

Imagine someone lying in bed doing nothing. Even in such an inactive state, energy is needed to breathe, make the heart beat, and drive all those countless chemical reactions which keep us alive. The rate at which these 'ticking over' processes take place is called the 'basal metabolic rate'.

How much energy is needed to maintain the basal metabolic rate? It is 35
difficult to say, because it varies from one individual to another. Very
roughly, the amount needed is 7,000 kj per day. This is about the same
amount of energy that would be needed to boil enough water for 100 cups
of tea. This figure applies to a person who is completely at rest. It doesn't
even include the energy she needs to feed herself. Scientists have tried to 40
work out how much energy an average person needs to get through the day
with the minimum effort, i.e. to get up in the morning, eat and drink and
do other essential tasks, but no more. The figure is about 9,200 kj per day.
A person could get enough energy to satisfy this need by eating one large
white loaf a day, though, of course, this would not be a balanced diet. 45

Few of us spend our days like that – most of us do something. Table 2
tells us roughly how much energy is needed each day by different people.

Table 2

	Kj per day
Child 1 year old	3,000
Child 5–7 years old	7,500
Girl 12–15 years old	9,500
Boy 12–15 years old	12,000
Office worker	11,000
Factory worker	12,500
Heavy manual worker	15,000
Pregnant woman	10,000

The amount depends upon the person's age, sex and occupation. A person
who spends most of the time sitting down needs far less energy than a very
active person. 60

What happens when we eat too much?

Suppose a person eats more food than is needed for producing enough
energy. What happens to the food left over? Most of it is turned into fat and
stored beneath the skin. The result is that body weight increases, and he
or she runs the risk of becoming fat (or obese). Obesity is caused by a 65
person's energy input being greater than the energy output.

The most 'fattening' foods are those which provide the most energy, such
as bread and margarine, cake and sweets.

How can a person lose weight? The only way is by making his or her
energy input less than the output. This can be done in two different 70
ways:

1   By taking more exercise: this will increase the energy output.
2   By eating less energy-containing food: this will decrease the energy input.

75   The first method is not very effective. A person has to take a lot of exercise to make much difference to his or her weight. For example, a man trying to lose weight may play a game of tennis for half an hour. In doing so, he loses about 700 kj of energy. After the game, he feels thirsty and has a glass of beer. The result is that he puts back all the energy he has just lost.

80   The second method is very effective if carried out properly. A person on a well-planned, weight-reducing diet can lose about 1 kg per week. Such diets contain relatively little high-energy food and a lot of low-energy food.

The best results can be obtained by combining both methods, i.e. by going on a weight-reducing diet and taking more exercise.

English Test

Reading Paper Energy for life answer booklet

First Name _____

Last Name _____

School _____

Write your answers in the spaces.

■ The paper is 1 hour 15 minutes long.

■ You have 15 minutes to read the Reading passages before answering the questions. During this time do not begin to write.

■ You then have 1 hour to write your answers.

■ There are 13 questions totalling 32 marks on this paper.

Answer the following questions.

Questions 1-4 are about Tiger Woods. (pages 2–3)

1   Underline the words from the following list which describe qualities that Tiger's parents taught him:

Concentration; selfishness; determination; craftiness; stability; recklessness; responsibility.   (1 mark)

2   Here is a list of events in Tiger's early life. Number them in the order in which they occur. The first one has been done for you.

1   Elrick Woods was born in Long Beach, California, in 1975.

His father tacked messages to Tiger's desk in his room.

He took up a putter and gave a perfect display of putting a golf ball.

He won a pitch, putt and drive competition against much older golfers.

He watched his father putt ball after ball into a cup.

He was out on the driving-range, using his father's 1-iron.

He asked for a 1-iron.   (1 mark)

3   What caused Tiger's father to be determined that his son would play golf well?

....

....

....

....   (3 marks)

4   The paragraph in which Tiger's father's tricks are described is linked with the one explaining his mother's role.
Write down the link sentence. Explain his mother's part in Tiger's upbringing.

....

....

....

....

....

....

....   (5 marks)

Questions 5-9 are about Jerry and his swimming.
(pages 4–5)

5 Before Jerry sank to the bottom of the sea, he felt a number of emotions. Underline two of the following feelings that he had:

      fear; jealousy; spite; horror; joy.   **(1 mark)**

6 Pick out and write down the short sentence in the second paragraph which most strongly describes the state of Jerry's nerves.

-- **(1 mark)**

7 Why did Jerry carry a stone with him as he got into the water?

-- **(2 marks)**

8 In the fifth paragraph, there is the short sentence, 'Victory filled him' (line 30). Here, the writer is using a metaphor: that is, the boy cannot literally be filled with 'victory' because it is just an idea, but the writer is expressing it that way, to strengthen the idea. Find two more phrases in the same paragraph where the writer does this.

-- **(2 marks)**

9 There was a great tension and excitement in the writing as Jerry struggled to swim through the tunnel and out into the open sea before he could breathe again. In the paragraph beginning, 'He drifted to the surface' (line 47), describe Jerry's feelings in your own words.
What does the reader feel at this point?

-- **(4 marks)**

Questions 10–13 are about the passage 'Getting energy from food.' (pages 6–8)

10 Words are often joined by a hyphen (we call them 'compounds') so that an idea can be expressed in a shorter, more effective way. These two compounds occur near the end of the passage. For each one, rewrite the same idea in your own words:

'well-planned'; 'weight-reducing'.

-- (2 marks)

11 Explain why a prisoner who is not allowed out of his cell does not necessarily put on weight.

-- (2 marks)

12 The author uses questions sparingly, but they occur three times at the beginning of paragraphs, at important points in the argument. Each time, there is no need to use a question. Why do you think the author does so?

-- (3 marks)

13 Do you think it is the author's purpose to persuade people to eat more low-energy food, and so reduce weight?

-- (5 marks)

ANSWERS AND EXAMINER'S COMMENTS
Reading Paper

Below you will find possible answers to the Reading Test questions, with the marks awarded for those answers. Compare your answers with those that are given to see how close you came to them and whether you would have achieved the same mark.

1 The words that should be underlined are:

Concentration; determination; stability; responsibility.

Total marks: 1 (All 4 correct)

Examiner's comment

This question allows you to show an understanding of the writer's use of language at word level, and to show an understanding of the passage by interpreting information at text level.

2 The correct order is:

1 **Elrick Woods was born in Long Beach, California, in 1975.**
5 **His father tacked messages to Tiger's desk in his room.**
3 **He took up a putter and gave a perfect display of putting a golf ball.**
4 **He won a pitch, putt and drive competition against much older golfers.**
2 **He watched his father putt ball after ball into a cup.**
7 **He was out on the driving range, using his father's 1-iron.**
6 **He asked for a 1-iron.**

Total marks: 1 (This order must be totally correct)

Examiner's comment

This question enables you to show understanding of the whole passage by selecting information from different parts of it.

13

3   **'Because he liked the game and he had big plans for his son.'**

There are 3 marks for this question, and this answer scores none because, although what it says is true, this is not the main or most important reason for Earl's wanting Tiger to play well. This answer also uses words from the passage, instead of the pupil using his own words. Therefore, there are no marks for this answer.

'Because Earl was keen on the game but he had long been denied access to the country-club world of golf because he was black.'

This scores 1 mark because although the important point about why Earl wanted Tiger to play well is understood, it is not clearly stated, and indeed does not mention Tiger at all. In addition, some of it is just copied from the passage, and so the marker does not really know whether the pupil understands the point. Although there are no marks specifically for the style, this answer is poorly expressed, as it is not written correctly in a sentence. Therefore, 1 mark.

'Earl Woods wanted his son to play golf well, because, as a black man, he had been kept out of the well-to-do world of golf clubs.'

This scores 2 marks because, although it is now correctly written in the pupil's own words, it does not mention that Earl himself played well, and it does not say what it was that he wanted his son to do. Therefore, 2 out of 3 marks.

'Because he was a black man, Earl Woods had been excluded from the comfortable, luxurious world of golf clubs, in spite of the fact that he played well. This is what made him determined that his son would play well enough to enter the golf-club world which had been denied him.'

This scores 3 out of 3. It is well expressed in correct sentences and mentions all the relevant aspects of the situation, including Earl Woods' motivation.

Total marks: 3

Examiner's overall comment

This question enables you to comment on the writer's purpose and viewpoint, as well as showing an understanding of the passage at sentence and text levels.

4   The link sentence is: '**While Earl handled the golf course and the playing schedule when his job allowed, as well as juggling the family's financial resources to help maintain Tiger's playing needs, his wife provided strength and stability at home.**'

There is 1 mark for the whole sentence. The whole sentence is the full answer because it balances the roles of both parents and is therefore the link.

'**Tiger's mother was a taxi service to get him to his matches. She made him behave himself at matches and taught him some of her own toughness.**'

This would score 1 out of 4 marks for this question. Three of the four roles his mother played are mentioned, but most of the phrases are copied from the text.

'**Tiger's mother ran him everywhere he needed to go to golf matches, and made him take part in family life. She insisted on good conduct, and taught him how to be tough when he was ahead in a match.**'

This scores 2 out of 4 marks. All the four roles that his mother fulfilled are covered, though in a superficial way, which probably shows only a surface understanding of the text.

'**Tiger's mother had to provide transport to and from his golf matches, and also made him play his full role in family life. She was also keen on him behaving properly and like a gentleman on the golf course. However, she did not forget to teach him to have a tough attitude towards his opponent at golf.**'

This scores 3 out of 4 marks. Each role played by his mother is described in the pupil's own words and the idea that his behaviour should be appropriate to different situations is introduced.

'**Tiger's mother was obviously a strong and well-balanced person, for not only did she work hard for Tiger in the sense of providing transport for his golf matches, but she also dominated him by insisting that he played a full role in family life, for which he would have to work hard himself. Under her watchful eye, on the golf course he would have to behave properly like a gentleman. However, because of her toughness, she taught him to remain highly competitive towards his opponents until the match was over, when he should resume being a gentleman.**'

This answer scores 4 marks out of 4. Each different aspect of her influence on Tiger is set in the context of her personality, and shows a thorough understanding of the passage as a whole.

The total mark for this question is therefore 1 + 4 = 5.

Examiner's overall comment

This question enables you to show an understanding of the writer's purpose and viewpoint, to interpret information, and to comment on the structure and organisation of the text.

5   **Fear. Horror.**   Total mark: 1 (Both must be correct)

Examiner's comment

This question allows you to show an understanding of the writer's use of language at word level.

---

6   **'His hands were shaking'** (1 mark)

The full sentence is required.   Total mark: 1

Examiner's comment

This question allows you to show an understanding of the writer's use of language at sentence level.

---

7   **So that he could sink** (1 mark) **more quickly** (1 mark) *or* **fast** (1 mark).   Total marks: 2

Examiner's comment

This question allows you to show an understanding of the writer's use of language at sentence level.

---

8   **'Sunlight was falling'** (1 mark)   **'a crack running up'** (1 mark)   Total marks: 2

Examiner's comment

This question allows you to show an understanding of the writer's use of language at metaphorical and sentence levels.

---

9   *Marks are awarded only for the* **feelings** *identified.*
It does not matter what else is said about Jerry or about the reader, and it does not matter how well the answer is expressed. It is only the descriptions of Jerry's and the reader's feelings that matter.

For Jerry: **weakness; tiredness; exhaustion; relief; happiness; a sense of achievement; fear ('His eyes must have burst'); desperation ('He tore off his goggles').** Any one of these scores $\frac{1}{2}$ mark to a maximum of 2.

For the reader: **relief; suspense; anxiety; continuing excitement; happiness; continuing tension; apprehension; uncertainty.** Any one of these scores $\frac{1}{2}$ mark to a maximum of 2.

No one will think of all the words for the feelings, and other words may be thought of and credited with a mark if the examiner thinks they are acceptable. That is why there is a maximum of 2 for each person.

Total marks: 4
(round up to whole marks)

Examiner's comment

Here, you can show an understanding of the writer's use of language at text level and an ability to empathise with the leading character.

10   1 mark for an answer which shows an adequate understanding of the compound; 1 mark for a thorough understanding; none for a misunderstanding.

Examples:

Well-planned: **'a plan is needed'** (0 marks)
                   'good planning' or **'planned efficiently and in detail'** (1 mark)
Weight-reducing: **'putting on weight'** (0 marks)
                   'taking off weight' or **'weight is deliberately lost in this way'** (1 mark)

Total marks: 2

Examiner's comment

This question enables you to show an understanding of the author's use of language at word level.

---

11   *The basic idea will be that a prisoner will have a low energy output, but will not put on weight if he eats low-energy food. Marks will be awarded according to how thoroughly this is understood and the detail in which it is expressed.*

'A prisoner who does not leave his cell will not put on weight if he eats low-energy food.'

1 mark here because both sides of the problem are understood, though the first is only implied, and there is little detail in the answer.

'A prisoner who is allowed no exercise will not put on weight if he eats low-energy food such as milk, eggs and vegetables.'

2 marks here because of a thorough understanding of the question and its answer, using material from the passage, with sufficient detail.

Total marks: 2

Examiner's overall comment

This question allows you to show an understanding of the writer's purpose and viewpoint so well that you can apply it to another situation.

---

12   *This question is awarded marks according to how well the pupil has understood the use of questions to mark the stages at which the author moves on to the next problem concerning the energy-producing capacity of food.*

Examples:
'The questions make you think about food energy' (1 mark);
'The questions focus the person's mind on the problems of energy-producing food' (2 marks);
'The questions concentrate the reader on the next stage of thinking about energy-producing food' (3 marks);

Total marks: 3

Examiner's overall comment

This question enables you to identify the author's purpose by commenting on the structure and organisation of the whole text.

13   *1 mark is awarded for the expression of an opinion, whatever it is.*

Either: **Yes, it is the author's purpose to persuade people to eat low-energy food.**
Or: **No, it is not his purpose to persuade people to eat low-energy food.**
Or: **The passage is purely factual, presented in an impartial, neutral way.**

Most marks are awarded for the evidence given in support of the opinion.
Not many marks would be given for big slices of the passage just copied down.
The way the facts are used determines the quality of the answer.

'The author persuades you to eat less, because if you don't use up the food, you get fat.'

This scores one mark because the idea is crude and basic, but correct.

'The author persuades you to eat less energy by saying what energy common foods have and then how much a person uses, so if you eat more than you use, you get fat.'

This scores two marks because the general idea is understood, but it is short and poorly organised.

'It is his purpose to persuade people to eat more low-energy food because he gives a lot of information about how much energy is contained in some common foods and then some figures to show the energy used by different kinds of people. Then he tells us that what happens when we eat too much is that the extra food turns into fat, and so we should eat less energy-producing food.'

This scores three marks. It is a better balanced answer, and includes the whole argument, but there is no detail, and it is not well organised.

'I think the author's purpose is not to persuade people in any way, but to present the facts about the energy produced by food and about how much energy is needed for an average day by people, according to age, sex and occupation. He does say how excess energy causes obesity, and how fat can be reduced by diet or exercise, but the facts are just presented, and he does not say obesity is bad, or try to persuade the reader to eat low-energy foods.'

This scores four marks. All parts of the argument are sensibly presented, with some amount of detail.

Total marks: 1 + 4 = 5

Examiner's overall comment

This question enables you to identify the writer's purpose by selecting evidence for it from different parts of the passage.

Overall total: 32 marks

Where to find more help

If you have not scored full marks on all these questions, then you will find lots of guidance on how to tackle Reading Test questions in *Collins Total Revision KS3 English*.

English Test

En

KEY STAGE
3

LEVELS
4–7

2006

Writing Paper

First Name _____

Last Name _____

School _____

- ■ Write your work on lined paper.

- ■ The paper is 1 hour 15 minutes long, including 15 minutes' planning time for the first task, the longer one.

- ■ There are two tasks.

- ■ The first task, the longer one, should take 45 minutes. This task has 30 marks.

- ■ The second task, the shorter one, should take 30 minutes. This task has 20 marks.

- ■ Plan your answer for the first task on the planning page opposite the task. This page will not be marked.

- ■ Write your answers in the Writing Paper answer booklet.

LONGER TASK

Game On!

Write the story of any physical activity in which you have taken part.

This could be anything, from a football, hockey, cricket or netball match, to skating or swimming, or a ride in a fairground or theme park, or just going for a walk.

Whatever you write about, include:

- thoughts and feelings you have before the event;
- a description of what you did;
- your feelings of satisfaction or pleasure which were produced by the activity.

(30 marks)

Use this page to plan your work. (This page will not be marked.)

Thoughts and feelings before event

-
-
-
-
-

What you did

What happened

Any problems or difficulties

How it ended

Feelings

-
-
-
-
-

Reasons for feelings

-
-
-
-
-

SHORTER TASK

A Walking Holiday

Imagine that you have a cousin who lives in a distant town. His or her Youth Club leader has written to invite you to join a walking holiday with the club for a week in August.

Write a letter to the leader, accepting his offer.

In thanking him for the invitation, refer to your cousin, who may be a boy or a girl, saying what great friends you have been for many years.

Tell him:

- what experience you have had of walking holidays
- what you hope this holiday will be like
- how you hope to enjoy it.

There is no need to set out the letter in any formal way.
Address the Youth leader as 'Dear Mr Lee'.

(20 marks)

Longer Task and Shorter Task

Pages 23–30 aim to help you mark, and improve, the answer you have given to the Longer writing task on page 20. Pages 31–36 aim to help you mark, and improve, the answer you have given to the Shorter writing task on page 22.

In order to work out what mark you would be awarded for each answer, do the following:

1 Read the **'Guidance on Key Features'** given for each **mark range**.

2 Read carefully the **sample answer** linked to each mark range. By reading all these extracts, you will see the improvement in the writing from one mark range to the next.

3 Of course, the **content** of your writing will not be the same as the content in the extracts, but you should be able to tell if the **quality of your writing** is similar.

4 Now see if you can match *your* answer to a mark range. If you are unsure, ask someone you can trust – your teacher, a relative or a friend – to help you.

5 Then award yourself a mark within the mark range. Choose a low mark if you feel your writing only just fits in the range and a high mark if you feel it is at the top of the range.

6 Once you have decided what mark your answer would probably be given, look at the guidance given under **'How to improve your answer'**. This suggests what you need to do to improve your answer so that you can do better next time, and achieve a higher mark. If you like, re-write your answer and then see if it fits the features described for the mark range above.

WRITING PAPER – LONGER TASK
Guidance and sample answers

How well did you do?   *3-9 marks*

Guidance on key features

If your answer deserves a mark in this mark range:

- You will have used full stops and capital letters correctly, showing that you can write in properly constructed sentences. You will also have used adjectives and connectives such as 'because', 'when', 'if' and 'although'. You will have used different tenses and even adverbial phrases (e.g. 'by concentrating hard...').

- You will have written a title and will have used paragraphs which begin with a topic sentence (e.g. 'I got excited about...') and which include some details of what you did.

- You will have begun the story by saying clearly what you are writing about. You will have written in the first person (e.g. 'I walked to the rollercoaster...') and will have described the event in some detail, mentioning some feelings you had, and especially some thoughts which finish off your story well.

Extract from a sample answer in this mark range

Gosthorpe Theme Park

In the summer holidays, we went to Gosthorpe theme park. It was the best day of the holidays so I want to write about it.

It is about twenty miles away and Mum and Dad decided we would go there because we did not go away on holiday this year, but just on day trips. There was a rollercoaster ride they said was the biggest in the country. Dad said my young brother, Jack, who is only six, was too young to go on it, but I could go.

I was excited about going on it, but a bit afraid too, because if I fell off I might have got hurt or even killed. When we got there, I went on it because I did not want to look scared by not going on. My dad paid and when I was on it, I was frightened, as it climbed slowly up a big rise, then I shut my eyes and held tight on to the metal bar in front of me when it looped round and we went upside down.

When I got off, my legs felt a bit funny but it was good being on the ground. I felt really proud that I had done it. My mum smiled at me and Jack looked up and asked what it was like.

"Okay," I said. "You will have to have a go when you are bigger."

24

How to improve your answer

1   Try to develop more of a sense of your own character by giving more detailed thoughts and feelings. Occasionally, use a simile or metaphor.

2   Use connectives to link ideas and events within the same sentence or between different sentences.

3   Try to use clauses to give more ideas (e.g. 'The ride was so exciting that I wanted it to continue…').

4   Try to vary the tenses, using adverbial phrases (e.g. 'By being determined…') or by the use of modals (e.g. 'I would have enjoyed it more, if I could have gone on it again.').

5   Make each paragraph lead on to the next logically by using adverbial connectives such as 'Luckily I hadn't eaten before I got on the ride…' Vary the lengths of paragraphs and sentences.

6   Use a good range of punctuation marks, including those needed for direct speech.

7   Use impersonal forms to increase variety (e.g. 'It was a testing time for me…')

How well did you do?   *10-16 marks*

Guidance on key features

If your answer deserves a mark in this mark range:

● You will have kept the reader's interest by such techniques as:
 – using direct speech
 – including details of your thoughts and feelings
 – including figurative language, e.g. similes or metaphors, to give some force to your feelings.

● Your paragraphs and sentences will be varied in length because you will have used connectives such as 'however' and connecting clauses such as 'When I felt this…'.

● You will have varied the verb tenses by using modals such as 'I would have been less scared if I could have got straight on…'.

● You will have used a good range of punctuation and will have introduced impersonal forms to add further variety to your expression (e.g. 'This was quite a challenge…').

Extract from a sample answer in this mark range

A visit to Gosthorpe Theme Park

I was extremely disappointed that we were not going away on holiday this year. However, I felt much better when our parents told me and Jack, my younger brother, that we were going on a trip to Gosthorpe Theme Park.

I had heard my friends at school talking about the new rollercoaster ride, the biggest in the country, and I wanted to tell them that I had been on it too.

When we got there, we went to the rollercoaster first. My stomach felt like a cage full of butterflies as I queued to get on. I would have been less scared if I could have climbed straight on without queuing. However, when my turn came, I got into the car quickly by being determined to do it. This was quite a test for me, because I used to be shy and weak, but this challenge had to be met.

As I sat down, I could not stop looking at the solid metal bar in front of me, and I grabbed it tightly. As we went slowly up the steep climb, I looked at the bar and took deep breaths. Then we went over the loop, and when we were upside down, I closed my eyes and put my head between my knees. I know that some people looked about and waved their arms, but they had probably been on the ride before.

Soon it was over and I got off.

"Well done," said Mum. "Jack and I saw you put your head down."

"Yes. Well, it's scary going upside down," I said, "but I will be fine next time, and perhaps Jack can come."

How to improve your answer

1   Keep a consistent narrative voice, tracing your thoughts and feelings, so that you can lead the reader through the story, controlling what he or she feels. Mix information with thoughts and comments.

2   Carefully organise the beginning and ending, to create interest at first and to produce satisfaction at the end.

3   Vary the length and structure of your sentences by using subordinate clauses and phrases to develop plot/thoughts/feelings. Sometimes, make the style more formal by using passive constructions (e.g. 'Customers were told to form a queue…').

4   Use a range of verb tenses, including modals, occasionally adding adverbial and noun phrases.

5   Develop links between paragraphs, and use a wide range of punctuation to give clarity to your narrative.

6   At the end of the story, try to bring together the different threads you have mentioned during the course of it. The story must have a deliberately organised shape and a number of strands in it to manipulate the reader.

How well did you do?

17–23 marks

Guidance on key features

If your answer deserves a mark in this mark range:

- You will have carefully shaped and controlled your story so that at different points you mention different threads. Having arrested the reader's attention at the beginning, and having regulated it throughout the narrative, you will have brought those threads together in a satisfying way at the conclusion.

- You will have kept a consistent narrative voice, mixing information with thoughts and feelings.

- You will have varied the length of your sentences by using subordinate clauses and phrases.

- You will have used a wide variety of verb forms and tenses, including modals in compound and complex sentences.

- You may have made the tone of your writing more formal in places by using passive constructions.

Extract from a sample answer in this mark range

A visit to Gosthorpe Theme Park

I hated my dad. He said that he could not take time off for our family to go away during the summer holidays and that we would have to make do with occasional trips. I was really depressed. What a miserable summer it would be.

It was not as bad for the others. Jack, my brother, was only six, and he hardly knew the difference between school and holidays because they often went on excursions at his school. Because my mum didn't have a job outside our home, her life seemed to me like one long holiday, although she said it wasn't. I was at secondary school, where we had to work so hard that I really needed a holiday.

Then, one day, Dad said that we could all go on a trip to Gosthorpe Theme Park. I was really excited. My friends at school had been talking about it for months. A few weeks earlier, the biggest rollercoaster in the country had been opened there. I was apprehensive about going on it, but, at the same time, I was determined to show the family and everyone else that I was not frightened to take a ride.

As we arrived at the park, we could see the rollercoaster dominating the scene, looming menacingly over the whole park, a sinister monster that was daring people to take a ride. Everyone who had paid was directed to a queueing area and my stomach was churning like a concrete mixer.

Suddenly, I found myself in the car, sitting on the hard seat, holding the front bar very tightly, and making steady progress up the steep incline before the loop. As I looked down, I hoped to see my family: I would have waved to them had I been able to spot them, but I couldn't. From the top, we plunged down into space, and a huge force, like a giant hand, forced us up again and over the loop upside down. Doggedly, I hung on as we careered up and down the rails and round bends that tried to fling me out sideways.

I walked on jellied legs to rejoin my family.

"Okay then?" asked Mum.

"Sure," I said with a confidence which belied my true feelings. "This is better than lying on a beach in some exotic place. I can't wait to go again and take Jack with me."

Now, I told myself, I had something to tell my friends.

How to improve your answer

1   Choose a deliberate style to sustain the narrative voice by which you are relating your thoughts and feelings about the event.

2   Continue to vary the sentence patterns by including a variety of subordinate clauses and phrases. Use a mixture of short, simple sentences, and compound ones.

3   Consciously structure the whole story by alternating between dialogue and narration, reflection and plot. Try to be succinct and imaginative.

4   Use a wide range of punctuation to give clarity and create specific effects, e.g. colons, dashes, semi-colons, ellipsis.

5   Keep the narrative viewpoint consistent, strong, effective and convincing.

6   Make sure the whole story is crafted, shaped and controlled for the interest and entertainment of the reader.

How well did you do?   *24–30 marks*

Guidance on key features

If your answer deserves a mark in this mark range:

- You will have maintained a consistent narrative voice, mixing information, an account of events and interpretations of your thoughts and feelings.

- Your punctuation will be very varied with a high degree of accuracy.

- You will have varied the sentence patterns with appropriate subordinate clauses and phrases. You will have used simple, complex and compound sentences to achieve specific effects.

- You will have alternated dialogue with plot, reflection with description. You will have imbued your narrative with an inspiring imaginative quality. Indeed, the whole story will have been controlled and manipulated with the purpose of giving the reader the best possible literary experience.

Extract from a sample answer in this mark range

A moment of triumph in Gosthorpe Adventure Park

I was in despair. I hated my dad. He had just told our family – Mum, my six-year-old brother Jack, and me – that he couldn't take enough time off work this year for us all to go away for a summer holiday. What a miserable prospect – the long, glorious summer holidays, and we were not going away.

Mum didn't work, and Jack seemed to play all the time at his Infants' school: it was me who needed a holiday. We were pushed so hard at our highly-competitive secondary school that I felt I really needed a holiday – "rest and recuperation", as our beloved form teacher put it!

Suddenly, the gloom lifted and the clouds of misery were dispelled. Dad had said that we could go for a day out at Gosthorpe Adventure Park, a theme park which had separated recently from its associated wildlife park and had considerably expanded. Among its recently acquired attractions was a new rollercoaster – the biggest in the country, it was claimed.

I had envied my friends at school, who had visited the park on the day the new rollercoaster was opened. It was, by their accounts, a terrifying ride – white knuckles, and hearts in mouths.

It did indeed seem intimidating as we approached it. It towered over all the smaller attractions, at once inviting and defiant. It sent out a challenge to everyone.

I felt the challenge very keenly. I had been shy, withdrawn and timid when I was younger, but now I longed to prove my adventurous spirit. Everyone was directed by stewards towards a narrow entrance gate. I would not have felt so nervous if I had not had to queue. My fear was in my mouth. My tongue was dry. I hoped I would have the courage to get in and hold on.

Then I was in the car, which was climbing remorselessly towards the loop. I looked down for my family, but could not see them. The sudden downward plunge took my breath away. An immensely powerful pressure forced us up again and we travelled the top of the loop upside down. Head down, eyes closed, I gripped the bar. We were careering along again, whirling round corners, and then screeching to a halt.

My dad was putting his arm round my shoulders.

"Was it worth it?" he asked.

"You bet," I replied. "That was better than baking on a beach."

"Well done!" said Mum, and Jack looked up wide-eyed.

"Can I come next time?" he asked.

"Of course you can," I replied, confidently playing the elder-brother role. And I thought of my new-found credibility at school.

WRITING PAPER - SHORTER TASK
Guidance and sample answers

How well did you do?   *3-8 marks*

Guidance on key features

If your answer deserves a mark in this mark range:

- You will have given Mr Lee a written acceptance of his invitation to join the holiday.

- You will have thanked him and referred to your cousin, mentioning that your friendship with him or her makes you sure that you will enjoy yourselves. As you will have written in the first person, your tone will be friendly. You will have been quite emphatic about your gratitude to him and positive about your hopes for a good holiday.

- Most of your sentences will be simply constructed and your use of full stops will be mostly accurate. A few sentences may have been expanded by using connectives such as 'when', 'and', 'but' and 'then'.

- You will have written in paragraphs and will have used some variations in verb tenses – at least the past, present and future tenses.

- You will have kept your vocabulary simple so that you will have spelt most of the words correctly, although you need to take care with words that sound the same, e.g. there/their; were/where; practice/practise.

Extract from a sample answer in this mark range

Dear Mr Lee,

I am writing to thank you for the invitation to join your Youth Club walking holiday. My cousin, Chris, had told me about it. Then I received your letter. In it, you told me where you are going.

I think the Yorkshire Dales is a beautiful part of the country, and I went there for a day's walk a few years ago when we were on holiday in Scarborough.

I want to tell you how very grateful I am to you for inviting me, because I am such close friends with Chris. We live a long way away from each other, and this will give us a chance to be together for a whole week. I like open air things, so I am sure I will enjoy it.

How to improve your answer

1   Give more details about yourself, your interests and character, and your hopes for the holiday.

2   Make your sentences more varied in length and construction, and increase the variation and complexity of the verbs (e.g. 'If we can cover twenty miles a day, that will have made me very fit by the end of the holiday.').

3   Keep the tone friendly and personal, and the style direct.

4   Try to widen the range of your punctuation.

5   Widen the range of your vocabulary by using adjectives and adverbs.

6   Clearly link your paragraphs, and develop the ideas within your letter.

7   Concentrate on spelling simple and common words correctly, especially words which sound the same, e.g. weather/whether; affect/effect.

How well did you do?   *9–14 marks*

Guidance on key features

If your answer deserves a mark in this mark range:

- You will have given the person to whom you are writing a fairly detailed picture of your character and interests so that he knows plenty about you before the holiday.

- You will have given a sense of looking forward to the holiday. You will have presented the information in such a way as to give Mr Lee an impression of friendliness and honesty.

- You will have varied the length of your sentences and also used a variety of verb tenses.

- Your punctuation and spelling will be mainly correct, and your vocabulary reasonably wide.

- Your paragraphs will be linked by a number of opening phrases, and there will be a development of ideas throughout the whole letter.

Extract from a sample answer in this mark range

Dear Mr Lee,

It was very kind of you to invite me to join the walking holiday which you have planned for your Youth Club this year.

As you might expect, my cousin, Chris, had already given me some details in a letter, telling me how the invitation arose in the first place. Chris and I are such great friends that I am sure I will have an enjoyable time with you, and that the other members of the club will make me feel welcome. I am really looking forward to it.

As far as the activity itself is concerned, you may like to know that I have taken part in a few sponsored walks of up to thirty miles. I have also been on camping holidays with other friends, and in general I am very keen on the outdoor life. Therefore, I hope I can contribute to the spirit of adventure and happiness that I am sure is characteristic of your members.

Please let me know of any particular equipment you would like me to bring, and let's hope the weather is sunny!

How to improve your answer

1   Use more complex sentences, and continue to vary the length of those sentences by using subordinate clauses and a range of verb tenses, including modals (e.g. 'I wouldn't have been able to…').

2   Continue to develop the links between your paragraphs by using specific devices such as temporal and causal phrases. Link ideas within the paragraphs by using connecting phrases (e.g. 'When I had done that…', 'At the same time…').

3   Organise your writing to give as much information, clearly, to Mr Lee as is necessary for him to plan your inclusion in the activities and arrangements for the holiday.

4   Use punctuation clearly to make the structure of your sentences clear.

5   Continue to make your tone informal and friendly, which is appropriate to a personal letter.

6   Spell complex and regular words correctly, but be very careful with words that are commonly misspelled, e.g. receive, brief, weird.

How well did you do? *15–19 marks*

Guidance on key features

If your answer deserves a mark in this mark range:

● You will have given Mr Lee enough information about your character, your interests and your likes and dislikes to enable him to include you in various arrangements and activities.

● You will also have linked your paragraphs by various devices, and connected the ideas within the paragraphs to give a sense of development to the ideas in the whole letter.

● You will have varied the length of your sentences and used a number of different verb tenses within them.

● Your punctuation and spelling will be clear and accurate.

● Bearing in mind that this is a personal letter, you will, by your informal tone, have given Mr Lee an impression of your friendly, open and honest personality.

Extract from a sample answer in this mark range

Dear Mr Lee,

It was very generous of you to invite me to participate in the walking holiday that you are arranging for your Youth Club this year.

Because my cousin, Chris, had previously explained by letter how the invitation came about, I had been anticipating your letter with some enthusiasm. I love long-distance walking, and can think of no more beautiful an area to do it in than the Yorkshire Dales. I hope we spend a lot of our time walking.

As long as Chris and I can be together, there is no possibility of my not enjoying the holiday, so close are our characters and outlooks. I have completed many sponsored walks, of distances ranging from three to thirty miles, and I have considerable experience of camping with my friends. I can be described as a team player, but at the same time, I am perfectly happy undertaking tasks on my own, if your planned activities involve this for different members. Whatever the arrangements you are making, I am sure I will play my role supportively and with relish.

Thank you once again, Mr Lee, for inviting me, and if you are able to send me details in advance of arrangements, regulations and equipment needed, I will do my best to comply with everything you require.

How to improve your answer

1 Ensure that you have given Mr Lee, and therefore the reader, sufficient information about your character, interests, tastes and experience to give a complete picture of yourself in the context of the potential holiday.

2 Continue to develop the way you vary the length and structure of your sentences, using a range of verb forms, appropriate subordinate clauses, and a variety of phrases. Both compound and complex sentences must be well under control.

3 Use as wide a vocabulary as is appropriate, but, at the same time, keep the expression succinct and economical.

4 Plan the whole letter from the outset, bearing in mind the number of paragraphs you intend to use, along with the phrases by which you link each one to its preceding one, and the way in which you will develop the ideas within each paragraph.

5 Make sure the punctuation and spelling are correct, being especially careful with irregular and complicated words.

6 Maintain and develop your deliberately informal style, and the engagingly personal and friendly tone which you have established.

How well did you do?   *20 marks*

Guidance on key features

If your answer deserves the very top mark:

- You will have given Mr Lee all the information which is relevant to the holiday. He needs to know something about your experience of such a holiday, your character and ability, and to some extent what you expect to do.

- You will also have developed the various aspects of style and organisation in letter writing to the highest quality that can reasonably be expected for someone of your age. Your sentences will be of varied length and structure, showing a range of verb forms and a variety of subordinate clauses and phrases. You will have used vocabulary which is exactly right to express all your ideas without undue elaboration.

- Your whole letter will have been well-planned, each paragraph linked to the one before. Ideas within each paragraph will be sequenced to produce a continuous development.

- Words will be correctly spelt and sentences correctly punctuated, using an informal style which communicates a friendly, personal tone.

Extract from a sample answer achieving this top mark

Dear Mr Lee,

I much appreciate your generosity in inviting me to participate in the walking holiday that you are arranging for your Youth Club this year. I am sure it will be an experience that I will value for many years to come.

As you will be aware, my cousin, Chris, had already written to me to explain how the invitation arose, and so it was with eager anticipation that I awaited your letter. I expect that Chris will also have told you that I love long-distance walking, especially in an area with all the natural attractions of the Yorkshire Dales.

The prospect of spending a holiday with Chris is one that I am greatly excited by, for we have so much in common in terms of character and outlook that it is simply not possible that I will not enjoy the holiday. Among experiences that Chris and I have shared have been family walking holidays, camping with uniformed groups, and sponsored walks.

I am sure that your members will make me welcome, as I usually relate easily and happily to people that I meet, and am able to co-operate with others within a group or undertake individual ventures if they are included in your programme.

I am so grateful for the invitation to join you, that I will be willing to adapt to any arrangement you make, and to comply with any regulations which are necessary. If it is convenient to you, perhaps you would send me details of any special equipment or clothing I might need.

I am really looking forward to meeting you and, as I said earlier, I have no doubt that I will enjoy the holiday enormously.

English Test

En

KEY STAGE
3

LEVELS
4–7

2006

Shakespeare Paper

The paper is **45 minutes** long.

You may choose to write about **one** of three Shakespeare plays:

- *Macbeth*
- *Much Ado About Nothing*
- *Richard III*

This paper assesses your reading and understanding of your chosen play and has **18 marks**. It consists of **one task** on two extracts from the scenes chosen for special study in each of the plays.

Turn to **page 38** for the *Macbeth* paper.

Turn to **page 49** for the *Much Ado About Nothing* paper.

Turn to **page 60** for the *Richard III* paper.

You have 45 minutes to write your answer to the following task.

MACBETH

Act 2 Scene 1 (lines 33 to the end) and Scene 2 (lines 1–40)
Act 5 Scene 3

Compare Macbeth's behaviour, attitude and language in these two extracts.

Support your ideas by referring to both of the extracts.

(18 marks)

Reading extracts for
MACBETH

In both these extracts, Macbeth is troubled by his conscience.

Act 2 Scene 1 (lines 33 to the end)

MACBETH   Is this a dagger which I see before me,
The handle toward my hand? Come, let me clutch thee.
I have thee not, and yet I see thee still!
Art thou not, fatal vision, sensible
To feeling as to sight? Or art thou but
A dagger of the mind, a false creation,
Proceeding from the heat-oppressed brain?
I see thee yet; in form as palpable
As this which now I draw.
Thou marshall'st me the way that I was going;
And such an instrument I was to use.
Mine eyes are made the fools o' the other senses,
Or else worth all the rest. I see thee still!
And on thy blade and dudgeon gouts of blood,
Which was not so before. There's no such thing!
It is the bloody business which informs
Thus to mine eyes. Now o'er the one half-world
Nature seems dead, and wicked dreams abuse
The curtained sleep; now witchcraft celebrates
Pale Hecate's offerings. And withered murder,
Alarumed by his sentinel, the wolf,
Whose howl's his watch, thus with his stealthy pace,
With Tarquin's ravishing strides, towards his design
Moves like a ghost. Thou sure and firm-set earth,
Hear not my steps, which way they walk, for fear
Thy very stones prate of my whereabout,
And take the present horror from the time,
Which now suits with it. Whiles I threat, he lives:
Words to the heat of deeds too cold breath gives.

[A bell rings.]

I go, and it is done. The bell invites me.
Hear it not, Duncan, for it is a knell
That summons thee to heaven or to hell.

Act 2 Scene 2 (lines 1–40)

[Inside the castle. Enter Lady Macbeth, alone.]

LADY MAC   That which hath made them drunk hath made me bold.
What hath quenched them hath given me fire. Hark! Peace!
It was the owl that shrieked, the fatal bellman,
Which gives the stern'st goodnight. He is about it!
The doors are open; and the surfeited grooms
Do mock their charge with snores. I have drugged their possets,
That death and nature do contend about them,
Whether they live or die.

MACBETH   *[Calling from a distance]* Who's there? What, ho!

LADY MAC   Alack! I am afraid they have awaked,
And 'tis not done. The attempt and not the deed
Confounds us! Hark! I laid their daggers ready;
He could not miss them! Had he not resembled
My father as he slept, I had done't.

[Enter Macbeth (with two bloodstained daggers).]

My husband!

MACBETH   I have done the deed. Didst thou not hear a noise?

LADY MAC   I heard the owl scream, and the crickets cry.
Did not you speak?

MACBETH   When?

LADY MAC   Now.

MACBETH   As I descended?

LADY MAC   Ay.

MACBETH   Hark! Who lies i' the second chamber?

LADY MAC   Donalbain.

MACBETH   *[Looking at his bloody hands]* This is a sorry sight.

LADY MAC   A foolish thought, to say a sorry sight.

MACBETH   There's one did laugh in's sleep, and one cried, 'Murder!'
That they did wake each other. I stood and heard them.
But they did say their prayers, and addressed them
Again to sleep.

LADY MAC   There are two lodged together.

MACBETH   One cried, 'God bless us!' and 'Amen', the other,
As they had seen me with these hangman's hands.
Listening their fear, I could not say, 'Amen'
When they did say 'God bless us!'

LADY MAC   Consider it not so deeply.

MACBETH   But wherefore could not I pronounce 'Amen'?
I had most need of blessing, and 'Amen'
Stuck in my throat.

LADY MAC   These deeds must not be thought
After these ways: so, it will make us mad.

MACBETH   Methought I heard a voice cry, 'Sleep no more!
Macbeth does murder sleep!' – the innocent sleep
Sleep that knits up the ravelled sleave of care,
The death of each day's life, sore labour's bath,
Balm of hurt minds, great nature's second course,
Chief nourisher in life's feast –

LADY MAC   What do you mean?

MACBETH   Still it cried, 'Sleep no more!' to all the house;
'Glamis hath murdered sleep; and therefore Cawdor
Shall sleep no more. Macbeth shall sleep no more!'

Act 5 Scene 3

[Dunsinane: inside the castle. Enter Macbeth, with the Doctor and attendants.]

MACBETH   Bring me no more reports! Let them fly all!
Till Birnam Wood remove to Dunsinane
I cannot taint with fear. What's the boy Malcolm?
Was he not born of woman? The spirits that know
All mortal consequences have pronounced me thus:
'Fear not, Macbeth: no man that's born of woman
Shall e'er have power upon thee.' – Then fly, false thanes,
And mingle with the English epicures.
The mind I sway by, and the heart I bear,
Shall never sag with doubt, nor shake with fear.

[Enter a Servant.]

The devil damn thee black, thou cream-faced loon!
Where gott'st thou that goose look?

SERVANT   There is ten thousand –

MACBETH   Geese, villain?

SERVANT   Soldiers, sir.

MACBETH   Go, prick thy face and over-red thy fear,
Thou lily-livered boy. What soldiers, patch?
Death of thy soul! Those linen cheeks of thine
Are counsellors to fear. What soldiers, whey-face?

SERVANT   The English force, so please you.

MACBETH   Take thy face hence! *[Exit Servant.]* Seyton! – I am sick at heart,
When I behold – Seyton, I say! – This push
Will cheer me ever, or disseat me now.
I have lived long enough. My way of life
Is fall'n into the sere, the yellow leaf;
And that which should accompany old age,
As honour, love, obedience, troops of friends,
I must not look to have; but in their stead,
Curses, not loud but deep, mouth-honour, breath,
Which the poor heart would fain deny, and dare not.
Seyton!

[Enter Seyton.]

SEYTON   What's your gracious pleasure?

MACBETH   What news more?

SEYTON   All is confirmed, my lord, which was reported.

MACBETH   I'll fight, till from my bones my flesh be hacked!
            Give me my armour!

SEYTON   'Tis not needed yet.

MACBETH   I'll put it on.
            Send out more horses, skirr the country round.
            Hang those that talk of fear. Give me mine armour.
            How does your patient, doctor?

DOCTOR   Not so sick, my lord,
            As she is troubled with thick-coming fancies,
            That keep her from her rest.

MACBETH   Cure her of that.
            Canst thou not minister to a mind diseased,
            Pluck from the memory a rooted sorrow,
            Raze out the written troubles of the brain,
            And with some sweet, oblivious antidote
            Cleanse the stuffed bosom of that perilous stuff
            Which weighs upon the heart?

DOCTOR   Therein the patient
            Must minister to himself.

MACBETH   Throw physic to the dogs! I'll none of it.
            [To Seyton] Come, put mine armour on. Give me my staff.
            Seyton, send out. Doctor, the thanes fly from me.
            [To Seyton] Come, sir, dispatch! If thou couldst, doctor, cast
            The water of my land, find her disease,
            And purge it to a sound and pristine health,
            I would applaud thee to the very echo,
            That should applaud again. – *[To Seyton]* Pull't off, I say!
            [To the Doctor] What rhubarb, senna, or what purgative drug,
            Would scour these English hence? Hear'st thou of them?

DOCTOR   Ay, my good lord: your royal preparation
            Makes us hear something.

MACBETH   *[To Seyton]* Bring it after me.
            I will not be afraid of death and bane
            Till Birnam forest come to Dunsinane.

MACBETH

In order to work out what mark you would be awarded for your answer, do the following:

1 Read the **'Guidance on key features'** for each mark range.

2 Read carefully the **sample answers** for each mark range. These provide an example of the sorts of points that would be made by a student working within this mark range. Of course, you will not have written exactly the same remarks, but you should be able to tell if the **quality** of your writing is similar.

3 Now see if you can match *your* answer to a mark range. If you are unsure, ask someone you can trust – a relative, friend or teacher – to help you. Then, within the range, decide whether your answer deserves the top, middle or lowest mark. Is your answer a very good fit within the range (top mark), a reasonable fit (middle mark) or does it barely fit within it (lowest mark)?

4 Once you have decided what mark your answer would probably be given, look at **'How to improve your answer'**. This suggests what you need to do to improve your answer so that you can do better next time, and achieve a higher mark.

How well did you do?   *3–6 marks*

Guidance on key features

If your answer deserves a mark in this mark range:

- You will have talked about Macbeth's behaviour and said how it is very different in the two extracts.

- You will also have noted that his attitude goes from being uncertain to totally sure of himself.

- You will not really have commented on the language of the scenes.

- Your coverage of the second extract will be brief.

Extract from a sample answer in this mark range

> In the first extract, Macbeth thinks he sees a dagger like his own because he is so worried that he is going to murder Duncan. Next, he thinks the dagger is covered in blood and then it disappears again. He does not know what to make of it.
>
> Macbeth is very nervous when he has done the murder. His wife has to force him to wash his hands and put on his nightgown. He is worried that he will never sleep again.
>
> In the other scene he is very confident and he gives all the orders. He wants to control everyone and he even orders the doctor to cure his wife.

How to improve your answer

1   As well as saying what happens in the extracts, bear in mind the different aspects of the task set (character, attitude and behaviour) and try to cover them all for each scene you are dealing with.

2   Use more quotations from the scenes to support your points.

3   This task relies on the big differences in Macbeth's behaviour from the earlier to the later stages of the play. Try to emphasise these.

How well did you do?   *7–10 marks*

Guidance on key features

If your answer deserves a mark in this mark range:

- You will have shown a general understanding of how Macbeth is different in the second extract.

- The relevant quotations you have used to support your points will show some awareness of language.

- You will have commented on the later scene but you will not have covered all aspects of Macbeth's behaviour as required by the task.

Extract from a sample answer in this mark range

> In the first speech, Macbeth shows that his mind is troubled. His nervousness about carrying out the plan to kill King Duncan is making him see things. He imagines there is a dagger in front of him but then tries to pull himself together, saying that it is "a dagger of the mind". The dagger keeps coming back, sometimes with blood on it and Macbeth is feeling ashamed of what he is about to do. After the murder, he is not feeling any better; "This is a sorry sight" he says when he shows his bloody hands to Lady Macbeth. She tries to shake him out of his worry, "Consider it not so deeply", but Macbeth thinks he can never stop thinking about it, "Macbeth shall sleep no more."
>
> In the second extract, Macbeth is far more confident. He makes all his own decisions and will not doubt himself or think or talk of failure. He does not care how he speaks to people and is very rude. He calls the messenger a "cream-faced loon" and "lily-livered". He also insults the doctor by saying, "Throw physic to the dogs."

How to improve your answer

1   Deal with both extracts at equal length. You could take each point you have made on the first extract and then say how things have changed in the later part of the play.

2   Where you have made a comment supported by a quotation, try to build on this by explaining how the quotation improves the reader's understanding. Use the point–evidence–comment technique.

3   The second extract shows that Macbeth is leading to self-destruction. Try to cover this aspect in your answer.

How well did you do?   *11–14 marks*

Guidance on key features

If your answer deserves a mark in this mark range:

- You will have focused clearly on several different aspects of Macbeth's character and behaviour.

- You will have discussed how the way in which Macbeth speaks shows his level of confidence, particularly in the use of sentence types.

- You will also have mentioned the importance to Macbeth throughout of supernatural signs, such as the vision of the dagger and the predictions of the witches.

Extract from a sample answer in this mark range

Macbeth's behaviour changes from nervous, uncertain and superstitious in the first extract, to confident, ruthless but still superstitious in the later extract. His uncertainty is shown in Act 2 Scene 1 where he keeps asking questions of the imagined dagger,

> "Art thou not, fatal vision, sensible
> To feeling as to sight? Or art thou but
> A dagger of the mind, a false creation,
> Proceeding from the heat-oppressed brain?"

In Act 5 Scene 3, Macbeth uses questions for a different purpose: he is assertive and the questions are rhetorical,

> "What's the boy Malcolm?
> Was he not born of woman?"

He also uses more exclamations which emphasise his passion and determination.

However, the supernatural elements are still in his mind and lead to his downfall.

How to improve your answer

1   Having identified the main aspects of the task, try to be more explicit about their relationship with the plot.

2   Where you make a point about the language, for instance about exclamations, make sure you develop it by giving examples and commenting on their effects.

3   Plan your answer carefully, as in a complex task such as this, it would be easy to miss out some aspects of Macbeth's character, attitude and behaviour.

How well did you do? *15–18 marks*

Guidance on key features

If your answer deserves a mark in this mark range:

- This is a coherent analysis of the task set, covering Macbeth's change of attitudes and behaviour, as revealed through his language. The focus on the task is secure, with no diversions into story-telling.

Extract from a sample answer in this mark range

Macbeth's behaviour is markedly different in the two sections of the play. He is initially hesitant, anxious, conscience-stricken. His speeches in the early scenes bear this out: he talks about his "heat-oppressed brain" and his "present horror"; he says, "I am afraid to think what I have done, Look on't again I dare not." This is in stark contrast with the later scene, when he is confident, ruthless and bombastic: "The mind I sway by, and the heart I bear, Shall never sag with doubt, nor shake with fear."

In the first extract he knows his deeds are evil and therefore must be hidden; his language reflects this: "Thou sure and firm-set earth, Hear not my steps, which way they walk, for fear Thy very stones prate of my whereabout." In the second extract, he shows no concern for the opinions of others, "Bring me no more reports! Let them fly all!" and his caution has completely gone, "I'll fight, till from my bones my flesh be hacked!" The language itself is brutal here, though there are reflective passages of desperate self-knowledge, e.g.

"I have lived long enough. My way of life
Is fall'n into the sere, the yellow leaf;
And that which should accompany old age,
As honour, love, obedience, troops of friends,
I must not look to have."

You have 45 minutes to write your answer to the following task.

MUCH ADO ABOUT NOTHING

Act 3 Scene 2 (lines 69 to the end)
Act 4 Scene 1 (lines 28–109)

> **In these extracts, show how far Don John controls characters and events.**

(18 marks)

Reading extracts for
MUCH ADO ABOUT NOTHING

In this extract, Don John voices his concerns about the forthcoming marriage between Claudio and Hero.

Act 3 Scene 2 (lines 69 to the end)

DON JOHN	My lord and brother, God save you!
DON PEDRO	Good e'en, brother.
DON JOHN	If your leisure served, I would speak with you.
DON PEDRO	In private?
DON JOHN	If it please you. Yet Count Claudio may hear, for what I would speak of concerns him.
DON PEDRO	What's the matter?
DON JOHN	*[To Claudio]* Means your lordship to be married tomorrow?
DON PEDRO	You know he does.
DON JOHN	I know not that, when he knows what I know.
CLAUDIO	If there be any impediment, I pray you discover it.
DON JOHN	*[To Claudio]* You may think I love you not. Let that appear hereafter, and aim better at me by that I now will manifest. For my brother, I think he holds you well, and in dearness of heart hath holp to effect your ensuing marriage – surely suit ill spent, and labour ill bestowed!
DON PEDRO	Why, what's the matter?
DON JOHN	I came hither to tell you – and, circumstances shortened, for she has been too long a talking of, the lady is disloyal.
CLAUDIO	Who? Hero?
DON JOHN	Even she – Leonato's Hero, your Hero, every man's Hero.
CLAUDIO	Disloyal?
DON JOHN	The word is too good to paint out her wickedness. I could say she were worse: think you of a worse title, and I will fit her to it. Wonder not till further warrant. Go but with me tonight, you shall see her chamber-window entered, even the night before her wedding-day. If you love her then, tomorrow wed her. But it would better fit your honour to change your mind.
CLAUDIO	May this be so?

DON PEDRO   I will not think it.

DON JOHN   If you dare not trust that you see, confess not that you know. If you will follow me, I will show you enough. And when you have seen more and heard more, proceed accordingly.

CLAUDIO   If I see anything tonight why I should not marry her, tomorrow in the congregation, where I should wed, there will I shame her.

DON PEDRO   And, as I wooed for thee to obtain her, I will join with thee to disgrace her.

DON JOHN   I will disparage her no farther till you are my witnesses. Bear it coldly but till midnight, and let the issue show itself.

DON PEDRO   O day untowardly turned!

CLAUDIO   O mischief strangely thwarting!

DON JOHN   O plague right well prevented! So will you say when you have seen the sequel.

In this extract, Claudio carries out his plan to shame Hero.

Act 4 Scene 1 (lines 28–109)

CLAUDIO There, Leonato, take her back again:
Give not this rotten orange to your friend.
She's but the sign and semblance of her honour.
Behold how like a maid she blushes here!
O, what authority and show of truth
Can cunning sin cover itself withal!
Comes not that blood as modest evidence
To witness simple virtue? Would you not swear,
All you that see her, that she were a maid
By these exterior shows? But she is none.
She knows the heat of a luxurious bed.
Her blush is guiltiness, not modesty.

LEONATO What do you mean, my lord?

CLAUDIO Not to be married;
Not to knit my soul to an approved wanton.

LEONATO Dear my lord, if you in your own proof
Have vanquished the resistance of her youth,
And made defeat of her virginity –

CLAUDIO I know what you would say. If I have known her,
You will say she did embrace me as a husband,
And so extenuate the 'forehand sin.
No, Leonato,
I never tempted her with word too large,
But, as a brother to his sister, showed
Bashful sincerity and comely love.

HERO And seemed I ever otherwise to you?

CLAUDIO Out on thee! Seeming! I will write against it.
You seem to me as Dian in her orb,
As chaste as is the bud ere it be blown.
But you are more intemperate in your blood
Than Venus, or those pampered animals
That rage in savage sensuality.

HERO Is my lord well, that he doth speak so wide?

LEONATO Sweet Prince, why speak not you?

DON PEDRO   What should I speak?
             I stand dishonoured, that have gone about
             To link my dear friend to a common stale.

LEONATO   Are these things spoken, or do I but dream?

DON JOHN   Sir, they are spoken; and these things are true.

BENEDICK   *[Aside]* This looks not like a nuptial.

HERO   True? O God!

CLAUDIO   Leonato, stand I here?
             Is this the Prince? Is this the Prince's brother?
             Is this face Hero's? Are our eyes our own?

LEONATO   All this is so: but what of this, my lord?

CLAUDIO   Let me but move one question to your daughter;
             And, by that fatherly and kind power
             That you have in her, bid her answer truly.

LEONATO   I charge thee do so, as thou art my child.

HERO   O God defend me! How am I beset!
             What kind of catechising call you this?

CLAUDIO   To make you answer truly to your name.

HERO   Is it not Hero? Who can blot that name
             With any just reproach?

CLAUDIO   Marry, that can Hero.
             Hero itself can blot out Hero's virtue.
             What man was he talked with you yesternight
             Out at your window betwixt twelve and one?
             Now, if you are a maid, answer to this.

HERO   I talked with no man at that hour, my lord.

DON PEDRO   Why, then are you no maiden. Leonato:
             I am sorry you must hear. Upon mine honour,
             Myself, my brother, and this grieved Count
             Did see her, hear her, at that hour last night,
             Talk with a ruffian at her chamber-window
             Who hath, indeed, most like a liberal villain,
             Confessed the vile encounters they have had
             A thousand times in secret.

DON JOHN   Fie, fie, they are not to be named, my lord, not to be spoke of!
                      There is not chastity enough in language
                      Without offence to utter them. Thus, pretty lady,
                      I am sorry for thy much misgovernment.

CLAUDIO   O Hero! What a Hero hadst thou been,
                      If half thy outward graces had been placed
                      About thy thoughts and counsels of thy heart!
                      But fair thee well, most foul, most fair! Farewell,
                      Thou pure impiety and impious purity!
                      For thee I'll lock up all the gates of love,
                      And on my eyelids shall conjecture hang,
                      To turn all beauty into thoughts of harm,
                      And never shall it more be gracious.

LEONATO   Hath no man's dagger here a point for me?

[Hero faints.]

BEATRICE   Why, how now, cousin! Wherefore sink you down?

DON JOHN   Come, let us go. These things, come thus to light,
                      Smother her spirits up.

[Exeunt Don Pedro, Don John and Claudio.]

BENEDICK   How doth the lady?

BEATRICE   Dead, I think. Help, uncle!

MUCH ADO ABOUT NOTHING

In order to work out what mark you would be awarded for your answer, do the following:

1 Read the **'Guidance on key features'** for each mark range.

2 Read carefully the **sample answers** for each mark range. These provide an example of the sorts of points that would be made by a student working within this mark range. Of course, you will not have written exactly the same remarks, but you should be able to tell if the **quality** of your writing is similar.

3 Now see if you can match *your* answer to a mark range. If you are unsure, ask someone you can trust – a relative, friend or teacher – to help you. Then, within the range, decide whether your answer deserves the top, middle or lowest mark. Is your answer a very good fit within the range (top mark), a reasonable fit (middle mark) or does it barely fit within it (lowest mark)?

4 Once you have decided what mark your answer would probably be given, look at **'How to improve your answer'**. This suggests what you need to do to improve your answer so that you can do better next time, and achieve a higher mark.

How well did you do?   *3-6 marks*

Guidance on key features

If your answer deserves a mark in this mark range:

- You will have summarised the plot accurately and relevantly.

- You will have told the story without emphasising Don John's part in it or without getting across the idea of 'control', which the task requires.

Extract from a sample answer in this mark range

> Don John starts off the rumour about Hero. He deliberately tells Don Pedro and Claudio that Hero has been seeing other men, so that Claudio won't want to marry her. He tells them that if they want proof, they can go with him that night to watch her let a man in at her bedroom window. They do not want to believe it.
>
> At the wedding, Claudio disgraces Hero by telling what he saw the night before. Don Pedro backs him up and so does Don John, though he leaves the other two to do most of the dirty work. Hero is devastated and faints.

How to improve your answer

1   You need to choose specific speeches of Don John's to show how he leads the other characters to act as he wants.

2   Try to say what effect his words might have on the other characters.

3   Consider whether the other characters are in any way to blame for what happens.

How well did you do?   *7–10 marks*

Guidance on key features

If your answer deserves a mark in this mark range:

- You will have shown understanding of Don John's control of the other characters, particularly Claudio and Don Pedro.

- You will have quoted relevant speeches and commented on them.

Extract from a sample answer in this mark range

Don John's accusations of Hero's unfaithfulness come right out of the blue. He first says, "the lady is disloyal" and Claudio shows by his reaction that he has no idea what Don John is talking about, "Who? Hero?" Don Pedro then really makes Hero sound very bad, "The word is too good to paint out her wickedness." He then promises to give them proof of her wickedness and says that Claudio won't want to marry her after that.

Sure enough, when it comes to the wedding, Claudio accuses Hero. He says, "She knows the heat of a luxurious bed" and everyone is shocked. As Don John has set it all up, he does not need to say much in this scene, and his speeches are short but to the point, such as, "Sir, they are spoken; and these things are true."

How to improve your answer

1   You might explain what we already know of Hero's character, to emphasise why the shock is so great.

2   You need to discuss how Don John suggested gently at first that Hero was unfaithful, then piled on the agony, so that by the wedding scene they were totally convinced of her guilt.

3   You might want to consider the reactions of Leonato, Beatrice and Benedick. Were they controlled by Don John in the same way that Claudio and Don Pedro were?

How well did you do? *11–14 marks*

Guidance on key features

If your answer deserves a mark in this mark range:

- You will have discussed the way in which Don John shamed Hero, leading to the abandonment of the marriage ceremony.

- You will have detailed which characters were most heavily influenced by him.

- You will have explained clearly, using quotations, the way in which Don John uses language to strengthen opinions.

Extract from a sample answer in this mark range

Don John carries out his plan to discredit Hero's reputation quite carefully. He begins, in Act 3 Scene 2, by asking Don Pedro if he might have a word with him. This immediately suggests that he has something important to say, making Don Pedro repeat, "What's the matter?" His message, of course, is really for Claudio, because he is the one who is going to marry Hero. Once he has made the accusation, Don John uses repetition to drive home his point: "Leonato's Hero, your Hero, every man's Hero." He then goes further, saying that he will show them the proof that very night. Claudio is completely taken in by his persuasion: "If I see anything tonight why I should not marry her, tomorrow in the congregation, where I should wed, there will I shame her."

During the marriage ceremony, it is also clear that he has convinced his brother, Don Pedro, that what he says about Hero is true. (In fact, Don John is using Claudio and Hero to inflict pain on his brother.) Don Pedro adds to the unfortunate scene by slandering Hero himself, "I stand dishonoured, that have gone about To link my dear friend to a common stale." Even Leonato begins to doubt his daughter, though Beatrice, Benedick and the Friar are not taken in by what Don John has planned.

How to improve your answer

1   Try to give an explanation as to why Don John behaves in the way that he does. This will add authority to your answer.

2   Compare the bare economy of Don John's language with that of the other characters, for instance, Claudio.

3   You might point out the drama of the climax by emphasising that it took place at a marriage ceremony, already a highly emotional occasion.

How well did you do?   *15–18 marks*

Guidance on key features

If your answer deserves a mark in this mark range:

- You will have given a coherent analysis of the ways in which Don John manipulates some characters, and thereby their actions, and his motivations for so doing.

- You will have commented not just on the language features, but also on their effects.

Extract from a sample answer in this mark range

In these two extracts, Don John plans and executes his revenge on his half-brother, Don Pedro, whom he secretly resents. He does this by devastating Don Pedro's best friend, Claudio – but those two are not the only ones to suffer, as the plot centres on destroying the reputation of Claudio's fiancée, Hero.

Don John begins to execute his wicked plan (first suggested to him by Borachio) by directly telling Don Pedro and Claudio that Hero has been unfaithful, "the lady is disloyal". While this idea is sinking in, Don John takes his accusation beyond doubt, "I could say she were worse: think you of a worse title, and I will fit her to it." Having maligned Hero in this way, Don John goes further, suggesting that it would now be demeaning for Claudio to marry her, "But it would better fit your honour to change your mind."

Having executed the first part of his plan, Don John proceeds to give his victims proof, "you shall see her chamber-window entered". By the time they are in the church the next day, Claudio and Don Pedro do the next part of the operation for him, by publicly shaming the innocent Hero. Cunningly, Don John remains quiet until he needs to press home his advantages, by endorsing the accusations made by Claudio, then by removing his brother and Claudio when Hero faints before they can change their minds.

You have 45 minutes to write your answer to the following task.

RICHARD III

Act 1 Scene 1 (lines 9–61)
Act 3 Scene 7 (lines 185–230)

Richard, Duke of Gloucester, who became King Richard III during the play, was a thoroughly bad man.

One aspect of his wickedness was his ability to deceive people, to mislead them by lying.

Show how he uses this ability in both these extracts.

(18 marks)

Reading extracts for
RICHARD III

In this extract, Richard Duke of Gloucester, after speaking to the audience about being a villain, meets his brother, George Duke of Clarence, who is being taken under guard to the Tower of London. Richard pretends not to know why.

Act 1 Scene 1 (lines 9–61)

RICHARD   Grim-visaged war hath smoothed his wrinkled front,
And now – instead of mounting barbed steeds
To fright the souls of fearful adversaries –
He capers nimbly in a lady's chamber
To the lascivious pleasing of a lute.
But I, that am not shaped for sportive tricks
Nor made to court an amorous looking-glass,
I that am rudely stamped and want love's majesty,
To strut before a wanton ambling nymph,
I that am curtailed of this fair proportion,
Cheated of feature by dissembling nature,
Deformed, unfinished, sent before my time
Into this breathing world scarce half made up –
And that so lamely and unfashionable
That dogs bark at me as I halt by them –
Why, I, in this weak piping time of peace
Have no delight to pass away the time,
Unless to spy my shadow in the sun
And descant on mine own deformity.
And therefore since I cannot prove a lover
To entertain these fair well-spoken days,
I am determined to prove a villain
And hate the idle pleasures of these days.
Plots have I laid, inductions dangerous,
By drunken prophecies, libels and dreams
To set my brother Clarence and the King
In deadly hate the one against the other.
And if King Edward be as true and just
As I am subtle, false and treacherous,
This day should Clarence closely be mewed up
About a prophecy which says that 'G'
Of Edward's heirs the murderer shall be.

[Enter George Duke of Clarence, guarded, and Sir Robert Brackenbury.]

Dive, thoughts, down to my soul: here Clarence comes.
Brother, good day. What means this armed guard
That waits upon your grace?

CLARENCE His majesty,
Tend'ring my person's safety, hath appointed
This conduct to convey me to the Tower.

RICHARD Upon what cause?

CLARENCE Because my name is George.

RICHARD Alack, my lord, that fault is none of yours.
He should for that commit your godfathers.
Belike his majesty hath some intent
That you should be new-christened in the Tower.
But what's the matter, Clarence? May I know?

CLARENCE Yea, Richard, when I know – for I protest
As yet I do not. But as I can learn
He hearkens after prophecies and dreams,
And from the cross-row plucks the letter 'G'
And says a wizard told him that by 'G'
His issue disinherited should be.
And for my name of George begins with 'G',
It follows in his thought that I am he.
These, as I learn, and suchlike toys as these,
Hath moved his Highness to commit me now.

In this scene, Richard Duke of Gloucester, surprised that he is not popular with the citizens of London, has decided to appear devoutly Christian. At first he refuses the offer of the crown of England when it is offered by the Duke of Buckingham.

Act 3 Scene 7 (lines 185–230)

BUCKINGHAM Then, good my lord, take to your royal self
      This proffered benefit of dignity –
      If not to bless us and the land withal,
      Yet to draw forth your noble ancestry
      From the corruption of abusing times,
      Unto a lineal, true-derived course.

MAYOR Do, good my lord; your citizens entreat you.

BUCKINGHAM Refuse not, mighty lord, this proffered love.

CATESBY O make them joyful: grant their lawful suit.

RICHARD Alas, why would you heap this care on me?
      I am unfit for state and majesty.
      I do beseech you, take it not amiss.
      I cannot, nor I will not, yield to you.

BUCKINGHAM If you refuse it – as, in love and zeal,
      Loathe to depose the child, your brother's son,
      As well we know your tenderness of heart
      And gentle, kind, effeminate remorse,
      Which we have noted in you to your kindred,
      And equally indeed to all estates –
      Yet know, whe'er you accept our suit or no,
      Your brother's son shall never reign our king,
      But we will plant some other in the throne,
      To the disgrace and downfall of your house.
      And in this resolution here we leave you. –
      Come, citizens, Zounds, I'll entreat no more.

RICHARD O do not swear, my lord of Buckingham.

[Exeunt Buckingham and some others.]

CATESBY Call him again, sweet Prince. Accept their suit.

ANOTHER If you deny them, all the land will rue it.

RICHARD   Will you enforce me to a world of cares?
Call them again.

[Exeunt one or more.]

I am not made of stone,
But penetrable to your kind entreats,
Albeit against my conscience and my soul.

[Enter Buckingham and the rest.]

Cousin of Buckingham, and sage, grave men,
Since you will buckle fortune on my back,
To bear her burden, whe'er I will or no,
I must have patience to endure the load.
But if black scandal or foul-faced reproach
Attend the sequel of your imposition,
Your mere enforcement shall acquittance me
From all the impure blots and stains thereof;
For God doth know, and you may partly see,
How far I am from the desire of this.

MAYOR   God bless your grace! We see it, and will say it.

RICHARD   In saying so, you shall but say the truth.

BUCKINGHAM   Then I salute you with this royal title:
Long live King Richard, England's worthy King!

RICHARD III

In order to work out what mark you would be awarded for your answer, do the following:

1 Read the **'Guidance on key features'** for each mark range.

2 Read carefully the **sample answers** for each mark range. These provide an example of the sorts of points that would be made by a student working within this mark range. Of course, you will not have written exactly the same remarks, but you should be able to tell if the **quality** of your writing is similar.

3 Now see if you can match *your* answer to a mark range. If you are unsure, ask someone you can trust – a relative, friend or teacher – to help you. Then, within the range, decide whether your answer deserves the top, middle or lowest mark. Is your answer a very good fit within the range (top mark), a reasonable fit (middle mark) or does it barely fit within it (lowest mark)?

4 Once you have decided what mark your answer would probably be given, look at **'How to improve your answer'**. This suggests what you need to do to improve your answer so that you can do better next time, and achieve a higher mark.

How well did you do?

3–6 marks

Guidance on key features

If your answer deserves a mark in this mark range:

- You will have given a summary of what Richard said.

- You will have given an account of what other characters did and said.

- You will not have pointed out how we know Richard is deceiving Clarence in the first extract.

- You will not have commented on how Richard's behaviour and speech in the second extract is not consistent with what he has done and said earlier in this scene and later in the play.

- You will not have used any quotations in your answer.

Extract from a sample answer in this mark range

Richard says how, now there is peace and no more war, he does not like peace and will amuse himself by stirring up hatred between people and playing tricks on them. When his brother Clarence comes by, Richard asks why he is being guarded and where he is going. Clarence says he is going to the Tower because his name is George and the King has had a dream about the letter "G".

In the other extract, the Mayor and Buckingham are telling Richard that the citizens love him and want him to be King, but he does not want this and says that he is not fit for it. But then they threaten that they will put someone else and not Prince Edward on the throne. When they lose patience with him, he calls them back and says he will accept what they want him to do. Therefore Buckingham answers that he is now the King of England.

How to improve your answer

1 Use short quotations from the speeches.

2 Do not just work through each extract from beginning to end, but pick out the parts that are relevant to the question.

3 At the beginning of the answer, state that Richard is good at deceiving people and say he has already arranged for Clarence to go to the Tower, but pretends that he does not know what is happening. Point out how Richard's actions and speeches are not consistent with his pretending to refuse to be King.

How well did you do?   *7–10 marks*

Guidance on key features

If your answer deserves a mark in this mark range:

- You will have included short quotations from both extracts.

- Each part of the answer will be relevant to the question and will not be just a narrative of events.

- The relevance will mean showing Richard's ability to deceive in action, relating to Clarence's journey to the Tower and to Richard's apparent refusal of the Kingship.

Extract from a sample answer in this mark range

Richard has explained that he is
   "Deformed, unfinished, sent before my time
   Into this breathing world scarce half made up."
Therefore, he does not want to take part in the "idle pleasures" of peace-time activities. He has planted suspicion about his brother, Clarence, in the mind of King Edward, and yet he pretends he knows nothing about it, while Clarence explains that it has to do with "prophecies and dreams".

By the time we have reached Act 3 Scene 7, we know what an evil and wicked man Richard is. Therefore, we also know that when he meditates with two bishops earlier in the scene, he is just putting on a show for other people who will be impressed. When he refuses to be King when Buckingham and the Mayor ask him to, this must also be just a show for other people. When he says, "I am unfit for state and majesty", he cannot possibly mean this because that is what his ambition has always been.

How to improve your answer

1   Quotations are now being used, but they could be built into sentences rather than used in a simply narrative way.

2   The answer is now relevant, but the quality could be improved by giving more detail and examining the subtleties of Richard's deception.

3   Try to build a stronger case against Richard by using better-organised expression of how unscrupulous his lying is.

How well did you do?   *11–14 marks*

Guidance on key features

If your answer deserves a mark in this mark range:

- Quotations will be a natural part of the argument, and will be built into sentences rather than standing on their own.
- More detail about how cunning and crafty Richard is will be given.
- The organisation of the answer will add strength to the argument about how wickedly unscrupulous Richard is.

Extract from a sample answer in this mark range

Richard has explained early in his speech that he hates the "sportive tricks" and "idle pleasures" of peace-time because he is deformed and has to proceed

"so lamely and unfashionable
That dogs bark at me as I halt by them."

He is therefore "determined to prove a villain" and in the pursuit of his villainy, he has fed suspicions about his brother, Clarence, into the mind of the King. Among these suspicions has been

"a prophecy which says that 'G'
Of Edward's heirs the murderer shall be".

For this reason, he cannot be surprised to see George, Duke of Clarence, being escorted to the Tower, but, pretending all innocence, he listens intently while Clarence explains an accusation made by the King which is based on "prophecies and dreams". Richard even thinks of other reasons for Clarence's committal, such as being "new-christened" or control of the King by Edward's wife. These, to the audience, are just transparent methods of deflecting guilt away from his own evil and sinister designs.

In the same way, in Act 3 Scene 7, the audience will realise that the sudden Christian devotion being practised by Richard, and his affected humility in declining Buckingham's offer of the crown, are devious ways by which Richard deceives people and conceals his own selfish and evil desires. This deception is never more blatantly obvious when he says,

"For God doth know, and you may partly see,
How far I am from the desire of this."

How to improve your answer

1   This answer is entirely relevant and well-organised. The way to improve further is to explore in even more depth how elaborate and effective Richard's deception is.

2   Select the best language of your own that you can think of, which expresses incisively and succinctly how sinister Richard's deception is, and how craftily and effectively he can mislead people.

How well did you do?   *15–18 marks*

Guidance on key features

If your answer deserves a mark in this mark range:

- You will have selected the most relevant and effective quotations.

- These quotations will be naturally integrated with your own sentences.

- The sentences will be built into a coherent, well-organised argument.

- By your analysis of how evil and elaborate Richard's deception is, you will show how thoroughly you have absorbed the play.

- Your ideas will have been expressed in such an incisive and thoughtful way that your answer clearly belongs to the top mark range.

Extract from a sample answer in this mark range

Motivated as he is by his own conspicuous deformity –
"Cheated of feature by dissembling nature,
Deformed, unfinished…" –
Richard announces right at the beginning of the play that he
"cannot prove a lover
To entertain these fair well-spoken days"
of peace, and therefore is "determined to prove a villain". The malicious and evil ingredients of that villainy are immediately seen when he explains that he has implanted seeds of hatred in the King's mind against his brother, Clarence. In doing so, he has used "drunken prophecies, libels and dreams" to poison the King's mind.

When Clarence passes by, escorted by a guard to the Tower, Richard pretends an innocent incredulity when the most flimsy pretext – the nomination of the letter "G" by a wizard – is explained. Because Richard has previously, in a soliloquy, claimed the invention of this fantasy, we know that he is behaving in a way that he has himself also claimed to be "subtle, false and treacherous".

Equally deceptive is Richard's sudden desire for Christian meditation with two bishops in Act 3 Scene 7: his bestial and murderous behaviour before this point has belied such piety. He even pretends to decline the offer by Buckingham of the King's crown, the desire for the acquisition of which has led him to scheme against and manipulate every character in the play up to that point.

69

When he says, "I am unfit for state and majesty", the audience knows that he is continuing the falsity and treachery that characterised his behaviour in the first scene. It is only the possibility that Buckingham will offer it to someone else that prompts him to recall him and accept his

"kind entreats,
Albeit against my conscience and my soul."

The audience by this time knows that the opposite of what he says is true, and he is showing transparently false modesty when he says:

"Since you will buckle fortune on my back… I must have patience to endure the load."

Then he accepts the office of King of England.